MW00490786

Contents

Sleep in a Strange House

Architect

Everyone I know I have put in a room.
They each have their own with a label on the door:

I am a door. I am locked.
I am occupied. I am alone.

When I find a staircase I didn't build, I am surprised.
Then I find more people – ones I've never met –

they too have rooms, but I haven't
a blueprint for these descending floors.

This Hour

– after a poem by Saskia Hamilton

When my children are still sleeping
the open window surprises
with ripe, orange-pink sun.
Is this hour just like all the early hours I've had?
A town outside revving up reluctant shoes;
the buildings blinking on their lights in rooms
redolent of talk, breath, and paper;
recently returned birds woke even earlier
before my dreams wove anxieties into film;
missing a bus in the dark, no lunch prepared
searching for a coat, an empty box of Ritz crackers
wouldn't fit me, but I wanted
the lady's brown suede eyelet one;
mornings I'd get a ride to school
in the tiny Volkswagen when I was late
the breath coming out of us in clouds;
mostly I'd walk, past the train bridge; a man would call us
on the payphone where we hung out together;
on our feet all day walking the concrete sidewalks
thrilled to talk to strangers and explore the tracks,
creosote burning up off the ties;
a friend's storefront windows, coffee and french fries;

our potential all coiled up like a snake's hiss
releasing bit by bit into the air
like little shocks, sparks, the sun on our hair,
the energy of parking lots, gasoline pumps,
just enough coins to call home;
and is this my home now; the one with hairs in the sink,
a build-up of skin cells, spit, and passive
aggression, love, smiles; and each child
with their own thoughts, sometimes told
but mostly kept silent;
how all our loves built us to now and rest at this hour
upon the sleeping heads of children.

This Month in Dreams

On my mother's lawn I watched a bird wedding. A white bird with flowing feathers and a crow were walking towards a hawk with brown grizzled feathers who was going to marry them. I went to tell my mother to come look, but by the time we went to the door, my cat had chased them away.

We were feeding white wolves. My husband put a piece of meat directly on the couch cushion (the couch was outside) and I vaguely thought *don't put meat on the couch*. The wolf came and devoured the meat. More came even though they didn't look exactly like wolves, more like wolfhounds. They were pure white. The fur was curlicued, kind of like the bride bird's feathers.

After that, we walked through the campus of a well-known prep school and students sitting in vans were indicating they belonged there by murmuring a low signal. A hum. A long poem was being studied. I read it out loud off the page. It was incredible. I can't replicate it awake.

As I arrived home I noticed three dead horses. One was in the road in front of my house, two were on the lawn. I looked up the meaning of dead horses in dreams later, and found out my marriage should be ending.

A book called "Myth" was displayed on the wall of an open closet space. It looked old. The word was curli-cued. The cinder block wall it hung on was painted green. There was an uncomfortable looking chair on the right hand side of the closet. As I looked at the space I thought there should be more books and a more com-fortable place to read. I also wondered if there was a staircase under the floor.

A Barbie doll was walking by herself across my curtain rod. The feeling was terror. I looked to see where she had come from. As if they had been molten as her feet touched the ground, her tiny footprints were metal stamps in the rug. A letter branded into each one.

Tammy Tommy

The library flooded.
Did you hear the sirens?
Friend I have not seen you,
didn't know how close you were to disaster,
the way the town is laid out.

Thank you for driving me.
The moon, a square
framed by linear clouds.

I show you how I make tarragon chicken.
You have everything I need,
the green apples and dried apricots,
their candy slice,
your scallion and lettuce.

We scoop the blueberries out of potluck muffins
with our hooked fingers.
We are that privileged.

You call to me from your individual sleeping tent,
resonant as spoken music,
that you hope you don't take on
the oily smell of your surroundings.

Push Your Fingers into the Clay

The boy says to the girl,
that's weird you're making a person out of clay.
People are not made out of clay. Meanwhile,
he is making a snail wedding with a minister snail
that fell off his perch and fainted. He has x's for eyes.

The boy's clay car is a phallus. He doesn't know this.
At the tip is a gun he makes by pushing an awl into it.
The boy with the snails says,
I will shoot you with a gun.

The girl says *you must really like snails.*
That's a really good snail you made.
Good thing the boys are here.

The girl says to the other girl,
will you invite me to your birthday party?

Only if I know you really well.
I am making a cake. I am making a heart
for my dad.

Then the other girl makes a heart
and a cake too with the same cookie cutter shape.

Mother and Child (with Father) on Airplane

She is teach, she is song, she is soothe,
he is asleep, he is comfortable, he is along for the ride
she is lap, she is table, she is distract,
he is headphones, he is entertained, he is distant
she is hip, she is bicep, she is wipe
he is eat, he is drink, he is self
she is bag, she is treat, she is breast
he is deep breaths, he is eye roll, he is looking on
she is ask, she is answer, she is up and down
he is drink, he is interrupt, he is tired
she is read, she is beg, she is plead,
she is wake, she is splinter, she is break –

A Cure for Dread

Hibiscus as big as your hand
pink as ballet shoes
you'd point your toes into
and gaze at the ribbons crossed
over your ankles' slim lines
to transform your feet into
something visible,

makes you want to leave,
drive away in your car.
You see yourself on the highway
a tiny dot from camera drone flyover.
There are women you know
who love the sound of their vacuums
picking up dirt – the snicking sound
clicks into their brains like the last
piece of a jigsaw puzzle.

There are life size dolls for men
who would rather not live with
real women. The perfect model
was created when supermodels

got too uppity. Too fat. Too hairy.
Webbie Tookay could never gain weight.
Her pixels were composed
of the best of the best –
Tyra Banks, but white. She would never
complain about payment or exhaustion,
could not see a flower and think: escape.
Could not see a flower and think.

I Imagine a Family Dreaming

The father dreams of being held down
under a heavy door he can't push off;
the weight like the sleep he can't fight.
It's like a tomb or the lid of his own coffin.

The mother dreams of a single candle flame
that multiplies, creating the spokes of a flower,
a breeze sets the petals to flicker
against the black night: a pinwheel, a ferris wheel.

The sister dreams a hot water bottle
the size of a throat lozenge is choking her,
then it's an eraser that rubs her head
until she disappears.

The brother dreams he is climbing the pine tree
outside his bedroom window. The higher
he climbs, the smaller the space
between the branches gets,
until the moon crosses to the other horizon
and he hangs by his knees.

I dream of a porch swing in the middle of a
field and empty landscape. The sun lights
the scene with an apocalyptic glow.
There are no people. There is no wind
yet the swing swings on and on.

Sleeping in My Daughter's Room

Cardinal notes pierce through the fan blades
into my sleeping daughter's room.
Her legs hang off the bed's side
and she cries out *Ow!*
so loud that I think she must really be in pain;
but she goes on sleeping,
hurting only in her subconscious.

Through the tree in the window,
morning light rips through leaf borders
like high heel marks on a sanctuary floor.
The tree, licked by a tongue of wind,
goes from convex to concave
and back again to its inherent shape.

Birds who Fell from the Nest

Tacked to the door is a picture of the door
and its hinges, its lock and keyhole
as if someone might need instruction
on how to open it.

.

A girl graduates to become
a corpse on TV. She flies up and down
into water on a bungee cord drowning,
breathing, drowning. I can't breathe.

.

There is a small bird on my tongue I have
put in there for protection while I search
the ground for others – sisters, brothers –
she is still egg-shaped and has foil feathers.

Venus

Walking alone along the beach road
at fourteen you have already been undressed
in the minds of men who slow down to whistle.

Full of fingers by the roses under moon,
and your head only seconds from the road edge.
Love does not become an equation you can calculate.

The odds of being injured
are the same as the impossibility of belonging.

Ocean water salty as your own soup,
you emerge on a half shell glad you look eighteen.

Owl Mother

Awakened by the whimper of my daughter then a sob,
I climb up out of sleep to find out her fear.
My heart beats hard, my body flushes hot.

Above my sleep I listen –
listen just below the surface
then it comes again and I detect a rhythm.

Who would do this? Why count the seconds
to the next sob and then the same intake of breath,
or is it an exhale? It's coming from outside.

Not my daughter after all. Relief,
and then to the window in my haze, listen, listen
and hope to help or know what it is.

This whoo whoo whoo
becomes the classic owl cry.
A rare sound for this suburb

and one I'd heard maybe once before
in the Maine woods one night
as I tried to sleep in a strange house.

I did not sleep all night that time when I was younger
and could leave anytime I wanted.
Still I chose to listen listen.

Sometime in 1997

Where you pull over on the overpass
a car wreck and a musician who lost
his playing hand (look there it is!)
and he won't let you help him,
afraid of bleeding on his
pink blanket you got from the trunk.
You're panicked, still counting on Daddy
to know the numbers by heart.
His answer to your voice
"Rachel?" gives away the other daughter you never knew
or a mistress all these years.
Your father's reluctant to call an ambulance
for this stranger you found
hand-less and delirious on the side of the road.
"He'll play music again. They always find a way."
The ambulance brings a tour bus too
with a tiny girl rollerblading underneath.
She does figure 8's around the wheels
like Tara Lipinsky.
The musician's son is severed at the waist,
(he has a son too) still alive
and after just having intestinal surgery

a week earlier, all scars and loose connections.
By the time the ambulance
arrives (and Lipinsky's bus) the family
has "pulled it together"
(the appearance of an unconcerned mother
does not surprise you).
The musician has a medical degree and assures you
he doesn't need to go to the hospital right away
as long as he keeps the hand taped to the wrist
(something about fooling the body).
Likewise, the child's torso is bandaged to his
hips and off they go for a walk,
ignoring the flashing lights,
the traffic they caused,
and your valiant attempts at rescue.

Dogs Riding in Cars

like overgrown animal children
silently watching the adults
who have taken charge of their fate
curly-headed
tall as a person
or short in the lap of the driver
or jutting their heads out the window
biting at the air loving the wind
waiting in the driver's seat
in the store parking lot
the dog wants to drive the car
or get ahead of the car
the dachshund who stands with his
front paws on the dashboard like
the figurehead on the prow of a ship
chest out at the helm
or the time I stopped the door
from slamming the beagle's tail
and crushed my finger instead
it's an absurd idea that we can protect
stop their death
or the one that sat in the car

staring menacingly out the open window
while I pumped gas and tried to look nonchalant
or the one that stood in the moonlit field
like some hound of hell
the night we looked for a camping spot
with bats flying up all around us
as our car flew away from there
but those ones that love riding in cars
break my heart with their eyebrows
and side glances
their bums on the seats
ears flapping then they're up
then they're waiting
until the engine turns over and they're off
do they want to learn to drive
run and run without stopping
if they could smile they would
it's that they don't that breaks my heart

Expiration

October seems just shy of orgasm,
a little death. Expiring in bed seems lofty.
Something about a last exhale,
an expulsion, the bellows do not open again
until the ragged breath of spring.
The fruited vine nipped by frosty
teeth bites. Rotting forestalled by canning,
or rotting anyway.

I can't keep away from thoughts of coming, going.
Dying, exhausted breath of August sweeps in
for some chicanery. Will it come again?
People carry on after someone is extinguished.
Miraculous! In their eyes, a waiting shadow
indicates involuntary breath, forgets it's a gift
or a burden, like remnants of tattered leaves,
little flags stayed in their brittle undoing.

Even the birds know what's at stake and squirrels
risk everything for the nuts trees drop in the road.
I do not know what's making that alarming sound,
but today I saw the biggest praying mantis
swivel its mechanical head to look right at me.

True Skies

The moon's a coin
half into its sky slot
as if it can't quite
commit to the call.

Janus-faced transitions,
the doors of war set to swing open –
am I coming or going?
I'm sealed for peace.

Does all water boil down
to an image of ourselves,
cloud vapor a stand-in for desire,
the pot red hot
and empty on the fire?

The moon's a lurking burglar,
embeds its jeweled self
between the tree trunks,
slips up even as we do
with our winked promises.

On the bridge over the muscular Piscataqua
the mouth of the moon shouts
in my ear; one of my faces turns
and I am up there alone in the light
like in black and white flicks
where something pivotal is about to happen.

I want to be the ocean at night in October

every star reflected off my back
a party light.
Stars drip into my curving waves,

engulf the magic sound of crickets,
slow soft sands and granules of light,
shadows that were footprints.

I didn't tell you yet
about the brine smell, the low horn
sounding far away,

but what of the dark things
the sleep deep fish
the swaying seaweed?

The chain of homes huddled close
each light on the horizon
a jewel in my necklace.

My waves lapping is not menacing,
of what they're capable, everyone knows.
I wait for meteors to shower

all I feel is the earth turning,
my feet planted in sand
that gives way beneath the subtlest movement.

What bird is it

doesn't want her own wings;
doesn't love calling out in code to her
family as they fly in formation?

I don't deserve my body. I should have
been born something else.
In dreams I welcome prosthetic legs

but, waking up this morning, I'm still with myself.
The sheets move when my legs tell them to.
What is this acute sense of being? I will be me

for the rest of my life. Will I look out
from my own face without knowing
what my expression professes?

My daughter asked what's my greatest fear
and I told her it was a loved one meeting an accident.
I might have said it's going blind,

but even the sighted can't see illness. Inside my own
bones, my organs turn bitter
even as I face the mirror.

After the Hysterectomy

"A day in which I don't write leaves a taste of ashes"
– Simone de Beauvoir

In the hospital
time became a wall with a clock I had to face.

Each hour was a stint of sleep
and pain that brought back childbirth.

At home, my dreams smelled of burning rubber –
I didn't care. Drowned

in the cold that seeped through windows,
the sludge of salt water that won't freeze.

No blanket could warm me.
I wrapped gifts in the basement,

against doctor's orders, overdid it. Wrote nothing
but notes on pills and bleeding.

Whatever was missing didn't concern me;
what was the point of any of it?

My childrens' first house was gone.
I pictured each baby curled up inside

deliriously thought: *you can't go home again.*
I had no affection for the place.

Strange how a woman creates
and then suddenly stops –

Lines Written in the Dark

Those crystal lit castles on the distant
shore and in front of me the lull and push

of waves shushing the shore lapping lake-like
and the lights blink on the horizon. The

waves make sizzling lines as they roll in
flashing electric light under the silver

full moon. Here there is the humid air
of stasis and verge, being and becoming.

Nantucket Sound is tricking me so quietly
I am on to the grift. The moon's intense

enough to cast a shadow of my head
rising from a straight back stretched

out on the sand, damp and flat. I am composed
of crushed shell and rock. In the middle

distance the sky cannot be separated
from the water except by the pinpricked

lights from houses cascading straight down
across the curve in the shore, reflecting as if

on stilts or echoing sound from a long way off.
Movement, a line of seaweed the waves left

like staccato dashes and hyphens. It goes
out from there to the vanishing point –

perspective and planes in front of me
a canvas of gray I know to be blue in the day.

Road Trip in January

One and a half hawks per hour
the sun is my spotlight
their heat lamp.
Sun feels good in winter
but on the way home I won't have that luxury.

I died looking at blackbirds
swarming trees;
I died thinking that tree was
pornographic;
I died even though I took all
necessary precautions.

I died with a billboard in my eyes;
I died while a funeral had just taken place;
I died but the sun still warms you;
I died and you posted my coffin on Facebook;
I died and left your anger;
I died and my neighbor's daughter's
husband was really broken up about it.

What are all these weeds on the median?
This was a mill town
now it struggles against arson and drug wars
polluted rivers.
Who said the worst thing is death?
I felt before I died that all the roads
were sinking, seeking the center of the earth.

Woodman Barn Dream

The dream had a ghost
and I couldn't move.

No one moved but the little boy's ghost
whose blood dripped onto my neck from his wound.

His body lifted from the pond of his murder.
His blood tapped my neck.

The cold room was bare.
The snow in the moonlight

negative space like a photograph's birth,
hovering, no sound, but then:

the blankets creaked in their cold way
moonlight walked through unbroken window glass.

The mice in the field hid in their mice-ish way.
The owls flew on their silent silver wing span

past the porch, the trees, the pond,
to what I always knew was there.

The snow is gone from the lake's reedy shore
I wonder if I've gone too far.

How will I get back?
Why did the boy not come to me again?

Is it all he wanted to shine once more
like light filtered through film?

When the Zombie Apocalypse Happens in Nightmares

You are in the bathroom
when your wife is attacked.
You hear her screams mid-stream.

Will you cut it short to go help,
or finish up, realizing the only thing you'll
be able to do is watch her character's story arc
come full circle, to a beautiful end.

She was the one you could see go,
feel comfortable with her leaving.

You are left behind to sleep
with your head upon
the chest of a dog under bushes,
sharing the last can of Alpo
with the only remaining warm body.

She needed to get away from you for a while.
You gave her your blessing.
She opened the door,
which was when it happened.

This is before the power goes out,
and water stops running in the faucets.

But wait – as her screams freeze
the blood in your veins –
you realize that you would have to fight off
the rest of the undead
whose dumb instincts are triggered by sound,

clean up the blood from the floor
you used to sweep innocent dried mud from,
and when you've crushed their heads,
you'd have to pierce her brain before she turns.

Why bother? You can't stay here anymore.
The night is grainy as an old film –
bushes and dogs and dark grass, all you see.

Gone are the Days of Liniment and Washing Soda

New enemies control,
anoint my louder head-voices
with despair and want.

These crowds appearing
when I'm alone suggest menace,
a burden of weakness blackened to a sickness
of solitary confinement.

Elucidate the elusive
rock wall I have built despite the sky,
in spite of open air. In spite of freedom
I wander along walls,
my shoes inappropriate, soggy.

Here's a horror ending to the greatest movie
ever rendered in the subconscious,
submerged as it is in slumber
a fine grain to the film, and archived –

chiseled seemingly out of stone the one minute
and balloon-popping into empty air the next,
magically, until that stone wall rises again.

Banished to forgetting,
I am a wonder to myself.

Train Insomnia

Early spring, my sleep blasted
by the train's extravagance.
Newly opened window. Every
adjustment takes disturbance.

I think about obligation
and want to just walk away
into the night, my form diminishing
like the lonely sound
even sleeping ears must be hearing.

What if we all came out
to protest the horn –
the moon and stars reflecting
the sun smell long gone from our hair –
but since we were already up,
decided the night's music was "our song"?

The rhythmic peepers sing down at the river;
the arc of night still standing sacred
as we link arms across the tracks
and sing louder than any machinery.

Spring

It's all of a sudden: unmoored
expanding, shrinking.
How do the bugs know when to start work?
A pile of dirt closely observed
becomes one moving mass of ants.
Snow still hides in discreet black piles
in the northern shade of buildings
but people come out, winter skin exposed
under shorts, tanks.
Sky, pink wisp and blue foam
behind the vees of still stark branches,
the bracken of their thorns.
Triangles of roofs survived
three-plus feet of snow.
Dead leaves still falling
inappropriately –
then nostalgia hits.
I remember my little boy in a photo – wearing
a blue jean jacket on an early April day
red cheeked, wind in his hair.
I remember my pre-teen self,
my Keds and the cracks in the sidewalk

when the sun melted on my hair
and I could smell asphalt breath
and I could go anywhere I wanted
on my own power.

The Lump in my Throat Appears without Warning

I have seen the killed bird land so lightly
it doesn't bend a blade of grass
What once breathed with open mouth hitching
after the cat got it did not survive the night

I have seen a baby laugh at the feel of rain
I have seen a deaf baby hear his mother's
voice for the first time singing: *I help you grow*

I have seen abominations in nightmares
A fawn tugging a dying dog's entrails out as it cries
A falcon biting my finger so hard I could not pry it off

A father hold his son against a wall by his throat
Someone thrown off a building for being gay
Bog people with ropes around their necks

I have walked right past the homeless
I have seen sunlight sprinkled on blue water
I have seen the hummingbird's red throat shimmer

I have seen rapes in movies and in real life
I have seen a psychiatric hospital
I have cried my love for people

I hide from people
Sometimes I don't want friends or sunshine or care
Love makes me cry

Sorry if I caused you pain
I don't blame anyone for mine

The Zero at the Bone

– after a line from Emily Dickinson

Even the word has an O in it
The way we say O instead
of zero in a telephone number.
The bone itself when sliced
in cross section contains a zero-
shape filled in with marrow.
The stuff of life. Think of an apple
cored, a zero in space as you
cut it out. Or have you eaten it first?
Despite what I said, can you hear
the space as it enters your body?
I've heard it's painful to donate
and even more painful to need it.

Postcard From My Son's Bedroom

The walls are white; the bed, which broke
two of its legs, is white and because of the broken
legs, slumps to one side, creating an off-kilter
sensation. Two years ago he decided
the blue and green rainforest theme
of his childhood should be erased.
Blank slate maybe, on/off, binary,
black clothes in a messy closet,
drawers open and spewing black fabric,
blinds drawn always, sun pushing the edges.
The air conditioner's white noise hides
what might be heard if the windows were open.
Trees outside must contain birds, perhaps
the wind sighs, rustles the leaves.
He must remember the sound but blocks it out.
The bed and the pile of dirty clothes
smell like his sweat, a distinct pinch to the air,
salt and tears and sorrow. I touch his sheets,
damp cotton I meant for comfort, a bit stiff,
odor emanating from the wrinkled place
his body defines. He asked for a succulent
to clean the air in there. I keep forgetting
to add it to my list, a bit of green,
and soil, the damp earth of cure.

Nest

– after "Night", a poem by Louise Bogan

The warm nestled hatchlings
and currents of wing swept air
Where what is dead, stays dead.
Lull and drone of finch heart –
and what preys, preys silently.
The persistence of danger.

Were it not for downy denial
this bird might have flown.
Proximity crucial to survival;
a stage of knowing not yet known.
In the weak fledgling step
that leaves its woven home.

Where feather, string and grass
support and comfort now abandoned
and the ever warming daylight
burns longer towards parched lawn
to set before we go to bed.

Where little heads are only beaks open
like breathing is a punishment.
Where again the mother leaves
every time you draw near,
the nest sits by your door.

Do you remember?
You never saw them leave,
but when one day they were gone
your human hand touched home.

Dream Meteor

The meteor glides just above my head,
as I watch, it turns like a head,
it is a head with a face
as I'm yelling at my son:
Get the telescope! The eye of the meteor
picks out his eye through the lens
picks him to die. I just know
this is how it will happen,
that the thing he loves
will take him from me.

Thompson's Field

Don't you care about the leaves?
a blue jay's frantic blame
on a sandy path with sweet fern.
In the sand, light
and the dust, shadows.

How we praise the wide expanses,
bend to the intricacies of goldenrod
the lace of lichen's paint
stippled up the cracked bark.

The living trees hold up the dead.
What will happen when I die
to those who would feel a loss?

I've lost my insomnia, let sleep
take over like a drug, like death,
like a mother's lullaby –
a preparation for death – comforts me.

Storybook toadstools
crickets timekeeping trill
the green seafoam of moss
the questioning depth of wind

moving away from tension
the worry of a lost dog
a shatter of wood and grounded cones
a tripping root, berries that might be poison.

How many more times will I miss the sun rise
already passed like the dog
whose claws left a kind
of cuneiform in the sand
or the birdsong I'm hearing now
for what seems like the first time.

How the sun draws out memory –
the wax blue of bayberry
crushed between its fingers.

Song at the End of Summer

When the mown grass stops greening
and my unwashed hands go clean
when the river begins its icing
and your sigh has left my ear
(you can love it all you want,
the earth does not love you)
but when my unbroken body starts mending
it will accept me, teeth and bone.
(know these words appeared in my sleep
and now they're all but gone.)

After Reading Plath

Late afternoon, you're gone
and I'm exhausted.
I walk out because I feel
like it, the outer skirts of
Hurricane Jose color the sky
lavender and watercolor gray.

Things that touch you and I
leave. Things you notice
and love their memory.
How would you remember me?
The proud, disappointed self.

Last night our daughter
had been crying, afraid
of hurricanes. I dreamt
of a woman with wild hair
who stared me into a closet.
I woke up and you were gone.
The woman was mad, clearly.
Nothing disturbs me quite like madness.

Hurricane air has been touching us,
stirring up waves and frizzing
hair, making floors sticky and clothes
soggy. The sky at dusk was senseless
out of its mind, the lavender
tint of a white-haired lady's blue rinse.

Late afternoon, you're gone
and I'm imagining what I'd
be like alone and painted
across the sky. Would I stay mad,
heavy with humidity, tinged with color;
finally strong enough to head out
to sea and disappear?

In the Dream

In the dream of black doorknobs,
the desserts were chocolate discs
filled with mint cream.
In the dream of broken branches,
doorknobs were used to fix them –
they opened to hollow,
splintered passageways.
In the dream of stolen love,
I used your ribs for a ladder –
they snapped into dust as I climbed.
In the dream of the charred infection,
your tongue diagnosed my disease,
pierced the blackened skin
down my throat
revealing a white the color and shape
of the full moon.
In the dream of the wild chameleon
climbing up my bedpost,
its swivelling eyes glanced off me,
morphed to a cat-like biter
when I tried to cage it.
I drowned it, poured it through
a strainer and it was grateful.

Advertisements for Ghosts

Would you like death to be one long dream
you never wake to the light around your shade
crowded so is the air

Don't you want tea that won't sluice through
a piece of the sunset could be yours, apparition
gold or pink your loved ones want to see you as

Is your box cramped and dusty
ashes spread, did your family forget where
are you dreaming still

Good
do you long for a birthday suit
a new one

Are you seeing hallways or open space
is memory nothing but image
emotion dulls over time

None of these mediums were right
the elastic pulled to breaking point
where do you want to be

The pain so shrill there was nowhere to put yourself
walking through walls is a gift
phantom shadows become objects, books, ornaments

Remember the mummies they found
the photos and x-rays they took
the guilt you felt when you dreamed the wrong thing

Subways leading to unknown streets
people you feared in life
hiding in the shadows cast by streetlamps

You will never see yourself again
is that what you want
no mirrors here

Though sometimes you might be able to see inside
what was once your own mouth, its teeth falling out
remember tonguing the hot socket

Would you like to have had more life
or are you okay being done
your body was going anyway

Remember the recurring visit to your old apartment
your street got to by a highway
you follow its concrete curving out ahead of you

Signs indicating the right way or wrong
but still you keep pushing the gas pedal
feel your hands control the wheel

Rooms laid out the same but completely repainted
replacement phantoms using its phones
and playing music too loud for the neighbors

What would you give to run again on muscled legs
out that door and into a day whose outcome
you couldn't possibly predict

The Green of Growing Things

I spent my early morning dreams
washing emeralds out of cloth.
Their hard nubs began to dissolve
with a lot of scrubbing
under my thumb's rub.

Even the neighbor, an old man of 98 who
ran his lawnmower through the grass in our yard
and straight into the kitchen
was getting things done.

I had been on the screened porch where the boundary
between in and out was defined.
People had wanted water. I went to get it
but all the glasses were dirty.

Like a waitress I kept it all in my mind.
What everyone wanted, had asked for
as rivulets of green melted from the stones
like candy on the tongue –
it took forever and never got done.

Woke to read a poem about unborn
babies and heard my name. Scolded myself
for not having written it, but then solace –
other imaginations are at work –
their ink flowing and verdant.

In what room of the soul do moments go

In the kitchen, whose soup on the stove; whose table
with one chair turned as if one more thing to bring–

the way a mind skips, forgets, remembers again;
the salt, the spoon, something essential;

in what locked cabinet do the huddled teacups'
shoulders no longer rattle with passing steps;

whose abandoned ceiling has fallen on the mattress;
how does the floor fall away under no one's weight;

whose fingers key the piano's long silence;
what music is sung to the ears left listening;

what roads in the mind do the worst thoughts travel;
what pale underbelly passes over the roof's gash;

what eye locks on motion;
in what room of the soul do moments go;

patient tree roots nudge their knuckles toward
the brittle foundation; and the screen door bangs

Acknowledgments

I am grateful to the editors of the following journals where these poems first appeared:

Good Fat Poetry Zine (2018, Winter, volume 2): "True Skies"

isacoustic (2018, March 19, online and volume third print anthology): "After Reading Plath"

SurVision Magazine (Issue 2, 2017-2018): "Tammy Tommy"

The Wickford Poetry & Art Anthology (2018, Summer): "I want to be the ocean at night in October"

The Wild Word (May 2018): "Dream Meteor"

About the Author

Jessica Purdy has lived in New England all her life and currently resides in Southern New Hampshire with her husband and two children. Having majored in both English and Studio Art at UNH, she feels drawn to the visual in both art and poetry. She has worked as an art teacher and a writing teacher. Currently, she teaches Poetry Workshops at Southern New Hampshire University. She holds an MFA in Creative Writing from Emerson College. In 2015, she was a featured reader at the Abroad Writers' Conference in Dublin, Ireland. Her poems have appeared in many journals, including *The Light Ekphrastic, The Wild Word, Nixes Mate Review,* Silver Birch Press "Beach and Pool Memories" Series and their "Nancy Drew Anthology", *Local Nomad, Bluestem Magazine, The Telephone Game, The Tower Journal, The Cafe Review, Off the Coast, The Foundling Review,* and *Flycatcher.* Her chapbook, *Learning the Names,* was published in 2015 by Finishing Line Press. Her most recent book, *STARLAND,* was published by Nixes Mate Books.

42° 19′ 47.9″ N   70° 56′ 43.9″ W

Nixes Mate is a navigational hazard in Boston Harbor used during the colonial period to gibbet and hang pirates and mutineers.

Nixes Mate Books features small-batch artisanal literature, created by writers who use all 26 letters of the alphabet and then some, honing their craft the time-honored way: one line at a time.

nixesmate.pub/books

29104048R00042

Made in the USA
Middletown, DE
21 December 2018